Irene

Also by Dennis Cooley
this only home
The Vernacular Muse
Inscriptions: A Prairie Poetry Anthology (editor)
the bentley poems
passwords

Irene

a poem by

Dennis Cooley

TURNSTONE PRESS

Turnstone Press
607–100 Arthur Street
Artspace Building
Winnipeg, Manitoba
R3B 1H3 Canada
www.TurnstonePress.com

Some of the pieces appeared, occasionally in different versions, in the following and are printed with permission: *Border Crossings*, *Sunfall*, *Prairie Fire*, and *passwords: transmigrations between canada and europe*. Permission from House of Anansi Press to quote from *Sunfall*.

Turnstone Press gratefully acknowledges the assistance of the Canada Council for the Arts, the Manitoba Arts Council and the Government of Canada through the Book Publishing Industry Development Program for our publishing activities.

The Canada Council | Le Conseil des Arts
for the Arts | du Canada

Canadä

Front cover photograph of Irene Cooley

Printed in Canada by
Hignell Printing for Turnstone Press.

Canadian Cataloguing in Publication Data
Cooley, Dennis, 1944–
Irene
Poems.
ISBN 0-88801-246-2
I. Title.
PS8555.0575 I74 2000   C811'.54   C00-920104-1
PR9199.3.C642 I74 2000

in memory of my mother
Irene June Cooley

and for my family

acknowledgments

with thanks to Douglas Barbour, editor of the manuscript, for the fineness of his ear and the shrewdness of his reading

and thanks to Manuela Dias, designer, for the care with which she has produced this book, and the patience she has shown, always

a note on *Irene*

I'd been in Germany that summer. 1990. Teaching Canadian
literature. An adventure, it was an adventure. We'd thrown
ourselves into it, travelled all over the place. It was a summer to
dream of, a privilege beyond belief. We'd loved it, but we'd
increasingly looked forward to coming home. And when we
did—this would have been within a few days of getting back—
my sister Lynn called from Estevan. Our mother was on her way
to Regina for an operation. Cancer. It looked bad.

I'd been shaken, that summer, when I'd called my mother
and her voice had sounded so shaky. And then the letter from
her, Diane bringing it with her—the handwriting weak and
wobbly.

The night Lynn called I dreamt of my mother in hospital and
dizzying lights. We went to Regina. And learned my mother was
dying. I wrote bits & pieces over the next few months, and they
became the basis for *Irene*. I'd written a poem, *Fielding*, about my
father's death years before, and now one about my mother's
dying.

I wrote and revised and added pieces over the next few
years and this is what I've now got. In the interim it's taken on
some associations, connections with the Persephone story
perhaps most obviously. It's fairly narrow in tone and voicing,
but I didn't want to fiddle very much with it. The book, like
Fielding, is personal and close to me.

I wrote this because I needed to tell myself what it was to
lose my mother. I didn't want her to slip away, and I wanted her
to be somewhere, something more than my memory. And I wrote
because I wanted to tell someone, but I am not sure what it is I
need to say or why I want to tell you.

An elegy. It's an elegy.

> → less like a tribute,
> more like a reflection
> of sensation

stop your ramblin'
stop your gamblin'
stop stayin' out late at night

—"Irene" by Leadbelly

fly way —
an other season

:   the geese
again

up the meridians
chase their noise north
sounds sun sends them through

migrate on brains
so small it is
the weight in a few
postage stamps

wave after wave of them
so many & so strong
standing in your mother's yard
the earth tilts under
april 1

& there are so many
& their voices
cry from return

cold winds they flow into
veins they follow
so large so loose they lose themselves
could be yeast in water
a beautiful scatter of pebbles

blood lost in the body
& it drifts
migraine in the cosmos

birds stray across the earth its face
where it turns to & from
sun bright in it & then dark

where it turns
its face
dark &
then bright

the flight you are taking
       laterally   to Europe
the way letters go
         & later
    your flight back

                south
                north   west / east
                      east / west
                              north
                              south

    it plucks
  blood the in & out
    in a
          season

     a well you have dug
           you would have
      something
            to push

    darkness you swim through

    night filling
       the way water
 comes into the hole
 a cow makes in spring

           a well you have
           dug & now it is
               filling

    your mother in estevan
  you phone it is her birthday
  it is june you get the wrong day
          again
     her voice
  on the phone

Dennis Cooley

breathing
you can hear her
voice going
in & out

-curtains in your room
you are small & it is late
the darkness her voice
once held for you
& held you
like a gift she would
hear you
splash
& pull you out

frog you could hardly swim
darkness you swam through

germany, now you are old
a few miles from the Saar
where your mother's family lived
& the river turns through summer
the long curve reminds me of home

& there is a room

people could be there
where
silence is
so
still
you feel it
feeding
on your face

you could drown
almost

you can
            barely
      hear it

breathing
         darkness
   in &
      out

      all our lives

      dying
               mother
      our bodies under us
                     dying
               & drying

         july is over
               i have come
      back from germany
      & Lynn has called

         mere words
         mere words
      I would say
      they mur

               mur
                  only they don't

            so loud now
         under the silence
         someone must hear
         someone must know

Dennis Cooley

dream all night

this is a hospital
3 floors   all underground
\ lost in

lines & nodes bleep
bright electric network
neon veins or nerves perhaps
the nodes are that bright

trace over & over
not knowing
where i am
going or what
i am looking for

wake /
exhausted & stunned

in a few hours you will
go to Regina

& Lynn
the evenness of her pain it won't ever
let go quite how she waits
the way she touches you

still pivot on your own kidney
the insides gone berserk

Sharon & Laurel how wise
they are strong (Sharon
somewhere in her own distress(say
it might be better how

jagged your emotions
this too is what you have
been thinking
& never said

i do not know what i would choose
or what if I were you i would choose

the ragged shore we coast
mixed weather
- wind & sun

this is your mother
you grew up in her
love & her body once
a rumour in her blood

*blind fish in an ocean
stopped her blood*

sits up &
asks
what is out of
her body now
& in it

my dad
silly smile on his face
has he been drinking

Dennis Cooley

I-rene good night Irene
iRENE goo
od night
good night I-rene
good night I-rene
I'll see you-uu
i-in my dreams

years & years ago
my father   singing

all that affection
the silly smile

the world flows

into ripeness
the roughriders win
in their green
& young birds
fling themselves on air
trust they will not wreck
or flounder there

young men shirtless
mow the hospital lawn
the Canada geese
our children fed
feed in the park still

meadowlarks make mother noises
when Diane & I walk too close
horses edge to the fence, hoping

decades of drought
& now the prairies spread
green across
our faces

the window my mother
sleeps & wakes at
wakes & sleeps in

our awkward
comings &
goings

walking

you back
into life
our lives
walking

with you
the first

steps
you took us on
Sharon Lynn me Laurel
almost 50
years ago
we take you
through

walking backwards
& out
doors our lives
turn back on
words
brief as breath

we offer you
to walk on

Dennis Cooley

want to hear a secret

you said when we were small
you would tell us

a secret sure we said
we wanted
        to know
we were all ears

               all yours ex

pectant years & years ago ex
pectin gramma wilson who dug
the wax out of her ears
        bees zuzzed

                  & then you would
              lean over we were small

     herds around your mouth
we wanted to hear wanted to hear
a secret we wanted to know

         psststt you'd say
      buzz our ears like a solenoid

        now i can't remember the secret
          I've lost the secret
     you whispert in our ears
            where they listened
            beside the wood stove
            the kindling i chopped

     thought you would live

       so long   i would die

        before you,
      hardly   thought
       this , then

thought of   you
holding me   still
at   my death

still as threads in a shirt
no one is wearing
still as a table
no one is at

& there is no more time
there is no more time for time
though you do not know this
yet you will know & make room
find time & even then
there will be spaces
so much room we will fall in
& never hit bottom

the way in space you float
forever & there is no
up, or down

outside the hospital

smell of wheat
& barley

ripening

Dennis Cooley

weeding the garden I was

weeding the garden you say
little smile at yourself
you jerk out from dreams
box cars starting up

your hands on the bed
loose grasshoppers

          & when you dreamt
          did you dream zucchini
    hung from their umbilical cords
    the smooth freckled skin
    buttoned on the end

were there poppies along the sidewalk
corn the kids would feast upon
our milk cow who leapt the fence
    the slow strong bang
        up to her ears in corn
the cow we called crescent jumped the moon shook
the long slow jolt she was up to her ears covered
with shit swishing it swishing mosquitoes we thought
in the near dark at the bottom of the garden
somebody was stealing ears off the corn
       & in the window a purple flower
      turning the light
         you turn at
      the garden of your face
      when i think of you

    did you dream needles & thimbles
    a table we would sit at
        out of the cold
        under the sun
       in the room
       in the garden

he who knows everything
does everything right
when it comes to gardens

his amazement when you yank
flowers by the neck
their colours startled in your hands
their eyes wide open under a hot sun
the middle of summer
this is you
jam them in & boom
there is a leap of yellow & purple
you surprise them into speech
know your pansies will come up
devoted as gophers

another time he passes
giant pumpkin seeds out
yours grows/
bigger & bigger & he grows
so astonished so perturbed you say
when Lorne hears this he's going to
shuffle off and shoot himself

that cells
tumble through
shirts in a clothes drier

thimble within thimble within thimble
perennial as thistles thick as stars
at the lake it's blue & summer
the whole world sticky with protoplasm

every year the ducks move
wind & sun & stars
pour their cells into other cells
life into life into life

Dennis Cooley

their calls tumble down
ducts in the sky
every April earth
unlocks in fall
they follow south
no one can know or follow

women give birth
daughters to daughters
their daughters too

Ukrainian dolls that go on
forever & ever
& there is always another
always a mother

Dec. 29 th /80

Dear Grandma,

We had a good
trip back too Winnipeg. Every-
thing was covered in frost.
Thankyou for the calligraphy
pen. I'm writing with it right now.
And thank you for the stamps.
I will try too write to you more
often. I know you c'ant write back
because of your wrist so I will
write to you until it's better.
Hope to see you soon

LOVE

Megan

string the room
with our attention
& at the end our love
hooked on a string

all day long
draw you back

what when
you know
will you think

you will want

mother tongue
        we learn
                to speak
        yearn to talk

    at our mother's breast
    we learn to say something
    you coax us into

            take our first
        shaky
                    steps
    into talk

walk on air
            again
        & again
            try to speak
                    our mother
            tongue tied
                    so to speak

Dennis Cooley

inside this room
      tied to you
we try &
        nurse you
back to breath

can hardly
      talk
hardly say
    a thing
dare not
     breathe
a word

talk in the hall

my mother
one night hears
the name cooley
talk of car wreck

everything confused
as winds in summer

fears that for hours

learn later you said
  there's this little old lady
  on her way to the operating room

you don't want any applause
until the doors are closed behind you

the time, inconsolable,
        I wept

boy who loves his father
        does his chores
wanting this for his father
his father's love

                the fork
        fallen under the hay
lost there
        & his father scolds

                        & later i father
                                impatient
                        scold my daughter
                                in her help
                        & she weeps

                        : the love she thinks
                                i have taken

        the time i wept
        & you sat beside me

        all the times i have thought

                i am dying for years it is
        my heart more recently cancer
                every pain that hits
                        it's cancer

                wrap my mortality now
                around a sore throat
                        when i hear
                        you are in trouble

Dennis Cooley

the throat closes
what we think
& feel there is no end
to what we do not say
there is no end mother
no end to want
or what we want

until you forget, dying
Dear Bea you write Nov 20
I'm ashamed when I think of
all the letters I've had
from you folks and
this is meant for all of you

the cancer has grown a lot
your clothes are too big
you have no need for a lot of clothes
Sharon helps you remember
        & Lynn does too

the page will say when I read it
I guess that I worry about what
the future holds for me you write.
Like you folks we mostly always
looked after ourselves.

months after you have died
your hand burnt to death
I can hear your voice, faintly,
                under

this is what i want

& cannot say mother

not though i know
you must know
& cannot say either

though i do not believe
i wish it so

that you may find millions of angels
blue as the skies we grew in
the blue cave the sky was
you called us by our names
when we were small
& you held us in your love
upheld us
perfect as milk in a spoon
like god himself
once did

goodbye Laurel

embarrassed as Megan
blushes when I kiss her
smiles
goodbye
goodbye goodbye
pleased

though she does not
can not   say

Dennis Cooley

I told him about the pain

I told him one side of me
felt thicker than the other side

      all he did was
      he put his
      hands on my face
         [like this]
and he said
      Mrs. Cooley

           you are going to outlive
             your family and all
              your neigbours

      & once

you were empty for your family
reached out with your voice
reached inside to find something
you left or might find

threw a net you hoped
would land over us lend us
what you found in your reach

      & I, impatient, said
      you don't listen
      & at once, ashamed
         felt the pain
      leap in you

      as if I had just hit
      a nail in wood

this is what happens, once

                                    we are small
                                    it is summer
                            or it is early summer
we are small, my sisters and me
we are sitting on the floor, playing
            this is at the farm
            it must be 1952
            it could be earlier

we are sitting in the living room
it is on the northwest corner of the house
there is a window on the north
a window on the west side
the windows are long and they are white
sun is warm on the floor
in the living room behind us
a large sheet of sun on the linoleum
the green couch is there against the wall
and part of the sun is on it too a corner patch
the radio is under the north window
it may be playing music

    Sharon Lynn and me
    we are sitting there, playing
    I do not know what we are playing
    but we are upheld in it

                        Laurel isn't there
                        maybe she isn't born
                        maybe she is asleep

it is the north window and we
look up, see a woman passing
right to left across the window
she is dressed in dark heavy clothes
though it is summer, or spring
we see, all at the same time, we look up

Dennis Cooley

watch the next window
my two sisters and I
she will be there and

she is she is dressed in black
a mouton coat and hat
she may be 35 or older (do I
know this then? and then she
passes the west window
I cannot be sure of the age now

we see this where we are
sitting on the floor in our living
room playing on the farm

run out to see who is this
first toward where
she would be coming
. nothing
,the other way
.nothing

& then again,
& again
, nothing
. in any direction

my mother is
hanging clothes on the line
shirts & pants still heavy with water
where in winter she would
pull down long johns
frozen into gray carcasses

this is on the north-east
where the woman must have started
did you see anybody mom
no she hasn't but
we saw this woman walking
around the house

no she says no
she has seen nothing

all this on the north of the house
me in distraction who is
this woman and where is she
going where has she gone

it is summer
we are small
there is a woman, passing
in this poem there is
a woman
passing

yes that others have
died die now
for want of time
will always die
alone or banging
the gates of god

our lives
temporary as cups
we drop & break

ate the warm flesh
the crumbly cakes of yeast
ate it raw (

Dennis Cooley

coming home loving
the elastic fragrance
      the milky skin
swelling the pan

dough like a breast
      the sweet slow smell
rises to the touch   sun by the window
soft flour in which it will lie

left muddy tracks in the kitchen
you scolded: look at what you've done

first poems, feet all wrong

we would come & go

christmas summer some
times easter thanksgiving often

we would enter & leave
your life drove into & out of
calendars through calendars
      we revolved in the seasons
      doors on our lives
      falling through
      time   a collander

    i would be
  sometimes impatient
absent when you spoke
        or wrote
weevilled into other lives

          want now to call back
            call you back
         as if i had never been
             away

muffled whir

sounds of cardboard kids clack
over their tires only softer as if
it were pieces of carpet

circle the Plains Hospital
Lynn Diane me

grasshoppers rising
their lazy gossip

she is just a little girl
she is 9, maybe, or 10

climbs onto our bed
one morning we are sleeping
bursts suddenly into tears
i don't want you to die
cries out that time
before it is time
the inconsolable knowing

catches you by surprise
beyond any comfort
you are already beyond reach
mom dad i don't
want you to die

already she knows
you are dead
she knows
she is alone

Dennis Cooley

exhausted

                    & not knowing
        what to do
                what to say
            that too
                wishing
                you didn't have
        to face it

        none of it
            ever

lazy you said I'm so lazy
I don't get anything done

        all the time
cancer a mugger grabbing
you it wants your life

all that time the gardens grew
how did your gardens grow
the miles you walked past
        time its seeds trickling
            ticking in you
                for a little while
        no more than a tickle
            / defused
        or a long fuse

how can we say
time surrounded
you could hear it saw
you had time on your hands
realized you could only surrender
knew no way to refuse

you were too polite how could you
you had no chance to stop

the clock about to go off
could not get off its spinning
the alarm that would wake us
every time

you took a breath another
bean popped out
grinning in your yard

always remember
the stone garden
sun that comes up like thunder
immensity of sky density of grave
birds that inflect the sky
stain it with their quick lives
when they turn
spring snaps
their wings apart

the trees arthritic & stricken
wood so hard
they could be anthracite

Dennis Cooley

all winter long
hardly dare   breathe
try to drink
through narrow rings
they sleep inside
the small hill north of estevan
the heat turns
gravel heavy as those
it has shovelled in

sun shoves
them down
into hardness
turns them into darkness

the sweet sully of flesh
we pass through

all anyone ever said
& all any of us meant to say
the paper heart
the world passes through
like clouded water

hospital

as we walk away

looks   so gentle

, so quiet   at night

it is not fate nor is it
benign no more than the growth

that overtakes you no less
than the handful of neglect
the doctor brought you
stuck in a vase by your bed

anther: part of a seed plant that contains pollen
anthology: a gathering of anthers, a bouquet of flowers, a bunch of poems

when he should have touched you felt it himself touched you
as a lover might,
tenderly
)I think, later,
\ shocked

Lynn as we leave

her sister touch

& again
her
hand

such a terrible
gentleness

Dennis Cooley

one time you put me
into music & lights falling like rain

we would turn inside
we would turn counter-clockwise
i remember
every time you rolled into sight
on my right
my mom & dad
i wanted to whirl
out of the music & lights
turn off all the sounds & colours
turn them all inside out

so there would be you & me
& my dad
the light & the music inside
the bright music & lights
the rain your hands were for me

wanted to
splot against you
the way grasshoppers went on windows
when you went fast & you smelled wheat
smelled hot grasshoppers on the grill

farm boy on a wooden horse
goes round & round
goes up & down
all the small children
on a carousel
solemn & scared
hang on to the reins

afraid to say he feared the horses
the infrared eyes of cows & horses

the time you put me
into time & took me out

Irene

the view the huge open view

we can see from your window

immense sweep of land

sky so open it has only bottom
only room to be at home in

sun riding the shadow

each day

across the room

tempting to say

the world is a fire then
Heraclitus is right
        Hopkins too

& we pieces of newspaper
someone crumples &

Dennis Cooley

                   throws in
        fllu - uMpP
             catch fire
     we catch the fire

                   for a moment
                        we feel
                     our skin
                        & eyes

                   collapse fast
                           the pictures
                           all the words
                   small edges red
                   others watch into black

                           waiting to see
                   if we can see
                                   again
                   in the dark

                   the ease with which
        you dismiss the pain
        refuse to explain yourself

                   you will go on
        dismissing old women
        who leave their beans & lettuce

        only in distress and apology
        confess to pain so severe
        they cannot hide it finally
        who are they to bother
        with or bother you

it's only old women
in fear & hurt who tell
their stories, diffident
even as they slide
into a more terrible pain

know you let them in you have
opened the door yourself

how little you listen
or care what they say

you go back to a life
others leave though
they would rather not

my mother the naked pain
she has never
said such things
ever before in her life

you are well
paid & you never
apologize not once
do you, ever

on the way back

Diane saying

get off the road duck

hawk rises heavily

limp gopher, trailing

Dennis Cooley

AIDS victims
Peter Gzowski saying
we all are dying

but it isn't
the same
we aren't
dying

others are
& we are glad
we are not

& there is   nothing
we can do

I love you
you said

sweet old sun
forever young
in whose hands
we warm light
bulbs in spring

the currents touch
burn quickly
& then burn back

a place no one speaks
no one calls nothing answers
a number no one answers

not though the world rolls
forever no one will hear you again

not though we stand on shore
call till we too fall in
a huge dark ocean

its awful
silence
when it
roars

drags
all our voices down
one by one by one

& sometimes there are
thousands
at a time
it takes under

Dennis Cooley

all fall cleaning

the office the study files
shelves desks cabinets
wiping dust & flies off years

shuffle things till the world begins
to fall into some neatness
         how satisfying it is
detritus scattered at my feet

wipe up bits & pieces throw out
flotsam jetsam dropped in passage
  toss some, keep some

      how final it seems
      a friend says, alarmed
      knowing of you

   watching the wake

      & a friend writes
      not knowing of you
      it's 10 years years now
      since yr father died
      and 10 years since you wrote
      about him do you still dream
      about him he is still having
      dreams about his father. "He
      died Mar 12, I think 1974."

there is a small boy he is five maybe four he is dressed in darkness he is
  wearing brown rayon pants & shirt to match his mother has just
  bought

he is squinting into the sun light falls off his face onto paper he leans over
40 years later rubbing darkness from his eyes but now he is mad he does
not like these clothes does not want to be in the picture his eyes hurt

it is the end of a hot day the sky is open behind him except for the
pumphouse frighteningly small in the picture he is facing into the sun
into the camera the long shadows the 40 years you are holding fall out
of your hands as only in the prairie they could your own long shade
stands in you on the other end you want to take him into the camera

he likes the shadows how steep & strong the time you are sliding down
though he does not know this either nor why you want the picture or
that you are feeling time pressing with the sun at your back he does not
care you want this perhaps his hair is newly cut it might have been this
may be why he does not want this he hates the bits of hair on his neck

he knows there is a garden to your left outside the picture behind the
picture the corn in forests above him there would have been a garden
there would have been all you hoped the day you take the pictures and
behind you the days you dreamt this day that would ever enter

behind you at the end of the lane he will hear a voice a few years later a
clear voice out of the sky strong and clear this will be the end of day one
summer the large sun in the west bright bird in its nest every day forever
a door closing in shadow he will hear what it says he will ask did you
hear it too though when he is older he will not remember what it said
the voice though you will say no you did not hear when he asks you then

he will remember where you stood in front of the sun the small spot where
your body will begin to boil over you want to coax a mother's picture
from him he will remember there were long shadows distinct as faces far
as memory as slanted

                              there is sun in his eyes
                    where you stand in front of the sun
                         you have disappeared into over
                          -exposed to time & the picture
                              we never took of you

                          you went into the picture
                    before we fell out of your hands
                              & you were dissolving
                    turning to light, losing your shadow

Dennis Cooley

always love
the way sun susp
ends its
elf on end
up ends

Sept
embers hang on
a stem
season a stamen
once steamed with colour
days burnt
we follow into a softness
a stammer
the smallest scratchings

a writing on wind
she says
common as to
morrow thin
almost as the marrow our bones relinquish

under the sun under our wishes
the windows
fill up on frost
christmas grew bright & feathered on your bedroom window
all winter we breathed
put our mouths to the panes
blew   open
small Os in cold all winter
we breathed in the white forests

our breathings stumble at the glass
bright as cancer

Irene

fourth sign
the sun crosses the first month
June 21 to July 22. the day
we returned, the day you heard.

Irene June Cooley.

say in books you do not believe
they form shells they are so vulnerable.
    it may be a home
some place they collect

the moon, the moon rules
infancy and motherhood.

 i read the books
i read the signs

i forget a lot

the garden

            we wrestled in
            you & i
    & i
            10 was it
astonished you could

        beat me
so easily
            it seemed
there by the yellow brick
by the corn where we wrestled

Dennis Cooley

do they put you among machines
their large eyes staring
the way they watch, noncommital

people on the other side
behind the machines
house their health there
walk into it live in it at will

do you feel quarantined
wish people would walk
their health out from behind
walls and windows leave
some of their immortality behind

and when you are alone
does panic buzz in you too
the way that man said he felt
as if he had been thrown
against an electric fence
and I lie awake myself
at night thinking
I am dying

I do not know mother
all I see is your remarkable calm
know the leaves turn to dry leather
dust in early September
and you hold yourself within yourself
your death to yourself

me wondering did you think
what if there were a switch
you could reach in &
trip

& the days would slow & thicken
the days would be pears we buy now in fall
days would appear to you open into gardens
and they would bulge   with light
                    turn into corn & squash
more than the growth that overtakes you

                        & then night
                    would
        /blip by
                        , an easy heartbeat

                    thanks giving

            the fall night
        slams shut frost
bangs & bangs all night long wants in
night could be an abandoned building
doors swinging in wind

next day the yard is wet
a gentle slant the sun takes
you always loved & were touched by
the ferocity of estevan sun
its velocity you moved a life through
you spent your garden swimming in it
talking to yourself & the carrots
the tomatoes you took in every fall
orphans from summer

Dennis Cooley

next day the light the nights ruin
look it is easy i can keep afloat mother
tread the bright light in your garden
though the yard is empty of summer
you huddled many summers with
  every summer threaded there

and the house is empty of you
you are not here you are
under the frost they pull over
   a hospital bed
St. Joseph's where you bore each of us
where Dana & Megan were born
your feet purple with veins
 they could be eggplants
 they could be flowers
there by the window over the valley

anthology: a gathering of flowers
where they spun out the back window

  step out Sunday morning among
  plants night has squashed
  some bloated some limp
  a few of them slump like tired drunks
  the zucchini still there
  buttoned to the rinds they wear
   closer than underwear
  impervious to cold or do they
  only look that way under the slime

  tomatoes sag into their old skins
   blood in their throats
  the dirt dries under foot harder
  than ever heat could make it

     it is thanksgiving we are home
     you are not here you are sick
     & still you bestow on Diane
     carrots potatoes tomatoes
      the back yard falling
     a bombed-out building

Irene

into death we are filling
up with cold when we are home
we will eat what you have given
the sharp juice in our mouths

soon the garden will shine with frost
hard with cold, white as cancer

we are all one body

it's as if we are
                all one
        body

                a friend says

        & they rip
parts off

    we are left
in our torn bodies
                silently,
        screaming

Dennis Cooley

your eyes

how large
your eyes

the large brown of them
at thanksgiving
i look into your eyes
& you look back
steadily

the large
silence
, your eyes

may the lord bless
you and keep you
may the lord make his face
to shine upon you
and be

gracious unto you
may the lord lift up
his face   toward you
and give you peace

Irene

grew in you
at first a rumour
a fist in your body
the room you let to each of us
frogs we swam in your slough
taking on bones

for 3/4 of a year we swam &
for 3/4 of a century
almost you swam too

& now the fist
i form
in you forms

the pain in my stomach
& a friend i hear, today,
has cancer of the liver

back & forth
swimming at the old power plant we went
up & down the pool in & out of the souris
we were learning to save lives learning
to keep ourselves
from drowning

snow the white prairies
the whole expanse
1,000 miles of frozen grass & snow
bedsheet under which
small creatures lie
"nivation" said the man whose name was whyte
& himself stricken with cancer lies quietly under

Dennis Cooley

this is winter you lie under
your pain written
by a man who did not hear
a terrible undertaking
he signed himself con
signed you forever
to a winter garden
a devastating poetry he wrote

there under the gauze the airs become
the white bandages & sheets

you have taken a breath
deeper than time

this on remembrance weekend:

there is a blood clot
in the tunnel it flutters
hovers there /red scarf
blood gusts & breezes

they hope to melt with poison
they now call perfume
the red silk rustling inside you
whispers of romance
that would kill

it could be a cloud on a fence
it could be net stockings

fear if it breaks
it will go straight
to your heart
slip through

silk stocking in wind
innocent as a nightcap
catching the direction
stop all flight

that it will blow up
against the lung
when it hits
the way to breath
will take your breath away

only we know it doesn't
know the way to your heart
has no way of knowing you
are a woman of few vanities
it has no way of reaching
any corner of your longing
never to wear the red silk
where it flutters

a dying bird
just below your throat

the glove compartment
you are playing with the button
you are waiting in the car
you are going on a trip
your mother and father are taking you
there will be an operation in rochester only you do not know

you will die without it
they will cut you in half like the lady in the box
though you don't know that either
they will slice you in half like the lady at the fair
they will let the pain out, the wound that heals
the pig screaming
and hanging there a heavy white slab, after

Dennis Cooley

40 more years they will slice you the other way
pelvis to sternum your appendix blown
& your belly button disappears
you hung brief as a melon from
melanoma a small river nearby

            and when you get there you do not want that
you try to talk your parents out of it
you do not know what it is you do not want
and dana when she is cut will call to you
dad don't let them do this to me please dad
& you stand helpless against her fear against sewing
would lift her from the needle she needs

            but now you are 10 just turned 10
it is fall august you remember or later
        it is nearly freeze-up
the crops are a failure they are rusted out
your dad scrapes up the speed in dust turns it
        through a long red auger into bins so you can go
they are out of money they are broke you do not know this

        this in the '54 Plymouth
        it is blue *powder blue* we say
it looks like the chief of police's car
        you are in the car playing with the mirror
                        they are not
            there yet

    bang the button on the glove compartment
        do you use your thumb
or is it the side of your hand (you do that sometimes

        you bang the button
                it falls
            open your
                        shock when you see it
    you have unlocked something terrible you fear to know
your alarm and half knowing
        all that blood banging around
    you are going on a trip
                your collar bone is broken
        something is going to happen

Irene   47

in the dream i see

                every time
        the white spot at the end

                there is rotten snow
                in the ditches & a
        white spot there
                at the end
        & i cannot talk
                & i think
        do i see it up ahead
        or have i passed it
                have i passed it already

        in the morning
            time folds out
                        your hands
                like cards, fallen
            linen tablecloth

                    reading your fortune
                    here in the palm
                    purple ink on my hands

        the pencil i will pull from my pocket
        the grocery store 8 years later
        Dana is coming home from Chicago
            Irene Cooley   it says
        a long blue pencil

Dennis Cooley

Dec 3 and Sharon can barely
     get you up

and you can barely
     remember phone calls

you need letters Pat says
something you can keep
     yourself in

 something you can keep
us in—aberrant children
blown into fields & pastures

late for supper missing
sports day you say, fallen, confused

     yes I am late
          I am always late
     it is late my mother
     much too late

     & I am much too slow, too far
     though once I was fast I was young

     now I cannot even
               catch time
          time is too fast now
     already near the finish
          you there cheering
        we are at the fairgrounds
        there is a race & I am running
        I can barely keep up
          you are near the line
                    cheering

hello mom
        ,dennis

        you speak
                        briefly
        you who always love
                to talk
        Lynn says you are
                                holding on
                you are waiting
                        for your family

        pain your voice cannot
        keep out

                abruptly stop
                        i have to go
                you have to go now

        at the end of rain
                        everyone at the bottom
                children play in canyons
                dangle from crayon thoughts
        real as zucchini their whacky freckles
        slow total absorption with which they lie
                under sun under moon mark them
                with waxy speckles & stripes

                                red is for when
                        orange is for during
                        yellow is for ever
                        green is for beginning
                                blue is for now
                        indigo is for getting
                        violet is for bearing

                brown is for after

Dennis Cooley

stories of grand mothers who
call from large eyes out to them
bright as the nylon clothes they wear
cry out in small joys and madness

brown is for ever
after brown is for never

standing at the separator
its large bowl of milk
13-year-old kid
fresh from milking
the crank rolls round & round
the white rope spreads
the circle floats gently
above the spouts

a steady stream   palewhite & watery
sound of it against the pail
spills from the long spout
another   slow & yellow
the shorter one
all this
happening from discs that spin

metal stacked inside
heaviness
you love to heft
& feel in your hands
left hand on top
they come apart slightly
you lift & let them
settle back   so perfectly   into place

the sound the weight
the steam when your mother scalds
                    hand to hand   back & forth
you play like an accordion

                    is this saturday
        it could be   any morning
                    though it feels saturday
        unhurried   something to come

In order to retain the flavor of this butter, it should be
kept in a cool place, entirely away from vegetables and
other like products. This wrapper acts as a protection
and should be retained on the butter until used.

One Pound Net Weight

it is not long before we will leave
the farm though we do not know, yet
            the handle is turning
the feel of it all the way up the arm

                your mom is saying
        is there anything you want to know
                you blushing no no
        if there is you can ask

            the milk spills through
                    the milk unravels
                turns yellow slowly thickens
        on the other end & thin faintly blue
                        in the longer one
            spinning the discs
            are   heavier
            the large bright bowl on top
        your mother sometimes put dough in
                (the milk in it)
            is getting lower & lower

    in the barn where you lean into the cows
music of the milking high & then   deeper

Dennis Cooley

ping ping \ milk hitting the pail   then swish **swish swish**
the gentleness of cows whose flanks you lean into
smell of new milk the cows their warm bodies
    veins in your arms sticking out

      elsewhere in the barn
the birds are dead stomachs
    distended babies you
   and your friends have
  filled with death

   the rain he would hold inside

   his hands for you

   a friend

   brings a gift
   unwraps it, off-hand
   it's nothing she says
   so I might receive

   knows of you
   your dying

   a large purple flower
     glass circle
   lines so fine
   you can hardly see

tiny veins whose
colour the sun will bleed
crocus past its season

my friend says it makes him mad
they are so feminine
the flowers in glass

hang it at my window
its bevelled light

it turns
                    slowly
catches the light

large purple bruise
in the window

you   have   carried   your   death

with you all your life
carried it carefully as a flower for years
you cared for us let us sit in under

& then the explosion hits
                your body a sun
throwing off bits of life
sun spots, pollen

a wild growth,
            dying

now when you
let it
                go

Dennis Cooley

it will not
let you   go
holds on tighter than a crab

in hollow walls & hallways
it will hold you
wide-eyed angel
terrible in its hands
the white angel will take you
with it
ineradicable as a weed
fill you full
with unwanted yeast
it will never
leave you
it will not let you
alone

not though you wrestle
not if you bless
or curse it

Dec 24

bright   & cold
clear white morning

the city deep in snow
deep as sorrow

fill the feeders
so the birds can eat

little granaries
hang from the pine

seeds in winter

red lights in estevan
small hearts on the evergreen

is this when old women die

it is Christmas & you are home, again
it is when my cousin Barry died
it is also when Megan was born & Pat
& the Sandersons were married
this is when my grandmother died
the night before christmas &
all through the house

nothing though lights are
blue & red & green
the paper is too & in it
we have wrapped love
the way always you did
& we tore it open

it is cold

there is snow
we are driving inside winter
make small marks on the white
surface make our way home

it is cold mother
it is a cold rainy day in Jerusalem
& it is cold here
there is snow
the country is dying
soon they will be dying
in a hot & desert land

Dennis Cooley

this is what I would
say to you but won't

everything dying mother
winter driving
through you like a nail
except a small stain
is spreading a coffee stain
the road is rough & sun
dogs the most brilliant
most colourful i have seen
they could be rainbows
ahead & behind in the mirror
snow drifts across the road
run in a silk stocking

we are moving inside
sorrow tomorrow
may be different mother
today you are dying
today it is cold

you held forever for us
held us once, always

our lives
fatal as words
sat in your branches

you a green tree in a dry town

driving home

all the other times, other Christmases
another Christmas, another year
driving home:

Dec 23   100 o'clock
                              & sun bends
              the sky)
wet tongue on envelopes
  you put letters in

     fields flat as paper
     whites out the lines

        2 days to Christmas
         it is a rail
                    way & elevators
        cold with silver

                   a power line at Elm Creek
                                     & our breath
                       fallen silent
               blends & shines on windows
            a kind of shyness

              Diane Dana Megan & me
                 in our envelope of frost
               making our way
             mailing ourselves
                       home to Estevan

Dennis Cooley

Christmas

play canasta
curse our luck
the cards all falling
for the women
they have all
the luck

yes you say yes in the dark
room i sit beside you you remember
the woman when we were small
circling the house you can remember
that it is Christmas eve the tree is lit
& you can remember

in the bedroom
you sleep & wake
wake & sleep

admit to no pain

it is Boxing Day

how do we speak to you now
the slow swirl of morphine
    you jerk open
doors on boxcars, unloading
the words dissolving already
that held our flesh together

Irene

and though we sit outside light
there isn't darkness large enough
                    to keep you by

        your bed its sheet of snow
                your blue satin gown
        under the blue & rose blankets
        it is working its way up,
                , the frost

                        in this hospital
        you hauled us out of silence
                Sharon Lynn Laurel me
                ladled us like butter
                    sat by our beds
        said what mothers to babies say
            combed your voice out
                    singing us to sleep
                        into time

            the string we swung inside you
                before you lowered us
                        each into life

        sat by my bed in this hospital
        the first 10 years of my life
        the always surprise to see you
        so pleased when afternoon let you in
        it was as if you knew where I'd be
        where we all would have been would be grand
        parents cousins nephews nieces aunts sons
        daughters uncles mothers fathers
                    coming into & leaving
                this place forever falls
                        like rain

                    and you know now I think
                    I am sitting beside you
                    mouth so dry you can
                    not do what you want you can
                    breathe only with effort

Dennis Cooley

can you hear me mother
this is me

no one can hear me
I cannot hear myself

I am trying to sing
you a song though
neither of us can
speak well & we love
to say & hear

things fall away
we fall
away from one another

I am trying to sing
what sons to mothers sing
when they are dying

so much happens in beds

start there start others
start the way lives start
out of them so startled
they lose their footing
around them all the love
lost all the love left

it is here we touch
babies lovers parents
        meet in beds
& at them leave
        one
            another

when time takes
over talks us away
takes us away

we were just
getting started mother
we were just getting
                started

a blizzard blows in

& the highways close
nothing moves in or out
the breathing harder &
    harder the way
sometimes you wince
as if breath stabbed
you in the side

blood drops too & your heart
races to keep up

   the storm goes on
your mouth opens as if you
                would speak

        first there is flesh
                then words
                        /& flesh
            how close they touch
                then flesh again
                then nothing

        the white dark
    silence in whose envelopes
    we send brief notes

hoping they will
              be
        felt
          gently
      between the fingers
                   sweetly
            as rain
      between deaths

maybe ill be lucky

      on the way you said
      maybe I'll get lucky

you said to the maybe the operating
you said to the room when you went
operating said to the maybe door
he opened maybe I'll get the operating
get lucky you went you said you went when
maybe maybe you went to the lucky room
you said I'll get lucky you said maybe

so small you had to

hold me up   look
over there   there's your dad
there's Sharon
there's Lynn
that's Santa
there is the horse running
in the rain & there is wind
against running down there is
wind in our hearts

always you were there
your heart a cupboard we drank from

now there is nothing
we can do to hold you up
we try
to hold you
up in the light
hold you up in the night
where we are always
going where you are
so beautiful mother
so able to hold us yet
look mother you are
still there you are
a small light
we hold in our hands

Dennis Cooley

when they lose
            a leg or hand
                        they can still feel
                  where it was
                        think it is
still there

            a leaf they cut
            and for days after
they say
                  you can see
            the missing piece
a flash of bubbles and light

once you would
            hold us

      we hold our
            selves now

            so very
                  still

a long series of cries

                        - birds, calling
            at the door
a small white-haired lady
gawks from a cane

where are the white women
the deliverers from pain

        the white-haired man who is
always trying to escape to find
        a driver to take him home
            sneaks down the back
        stairs says to me asks me
            for the second time
                will it be tonight

    walk into the hall
        the smell hits
                : boiled turnips   or shit
        the smothering smell, thick
    always hated the smell of turnips
                        when you cooked

    Sharon says smell that
                    that's cancer
    but I didn't smell it in the room
            didn't know what it was

    you can smell cancer in the hall
            once you've smelled it
        you never forget
                    Sharon says
    there are three on this ward

                                    Dennis Cooley

he drained away
silent & heavy as a stone
you my mother so calm when you said
it's time & I came out of sleep
         & then he was dead
what can't ever be helped or stopped

my dad was a curling rock
    rumbled over ice
digging in & digging in
until at last
         he stopped
the ice was so heavy

your dying is
what I cannot say I have no
comparison nor can think of one

my sisters are
    calm   steady
Dale Lorne Don Diane
        the grandchildren

    inside your death
    it is noise it is spasm
    it is long   it is longer

you are quiet now
you are very quiet

& then you are dead

Dennis Cooley

to see you
   alone
you are so
beautiful mother

& yes as
Sharon said

there is   there
            is a small
smile on your face

hospital deposits
light onto snow
i walked through
on the way to school
      30 years ago
the place we empty into
out of your unasking

every spring my mother poked spring
her finger was a pencil
she wet & rubbed seeds off

in no time they were singing back potatoes
lettuce tomato carrots cucumber shouting
the whole yard a convention of vegetables
you couldn't sleep nights for their sighs & yelps
the frogs began to move
out they couldn't
hear themselves think
would have died off
if they hadn't moved on
their mating calls drowned
in the cries of onions

all summer long the garden littered
the vegetables were terribly literate &
they were talking
with my mom she'd read to them
at night at the table
file them away in the fall
under glass

out she'd go rain or shine &
there she'd be she'd
have them dead to rights she'd
come back changed even in winter
they would not refuse their small
breathings, murmurings, rings
& rings of murmurs they turned
& tossed in their sleep

maybe they were humouring her
seeds shining, thinking of mother

Dennis Cooley

we right ourselves with stories

      outside it storms
      the roads are filling in
      with wind & greed
      they are blocking up
      from cold & misery
      inside our mother's house
      we tell stories & we are laughing

the night is filling up too

      the hole
      filling with
      night comes
         into

      & i cannot
remember now

  were there
flowers at your
        funeral

inside I find your Christmas letter

you do not know what time you have
everyone has been home is coming home
& in your garden last summer you grew
the best flowers you ever had

so modest you were

always so modest
made no claims upon the world
or your continuance in it

I'm ashamed you wrote, dying
when I think of all the letters
I've had from you folks
& this is meant for all of you.

left as you lived
no admission of pain
no requests for yourself
the last months gathering
the small things of your life

you would give bits of jewelry
you would give us everything mother
& you did

Dennis Cooley

parts of what in the house were yours to keep
you kept us in, we came back year after year
you kept the house, we kept coming
this was your house you were our mother

so calm sorting things into your death
wrote one of the last letters
yes your hand is there, the ridged nail
down the back of your thumb
though the pain had shaken it for months

Christmas eve   the bitter cold
you asked when I sat with you
was it rain we heard at the window

I love you

you said
I love you

thinking now
you are dead
childhood stole
our daughters from you
the slouch of pubescence & cities

the splash of aunts & sun
one time zone apart
2 provinces side by side
a line on a sheet of paper
every summer time happened
thinner than ozone & as lethal

there must have been times
the ozone seemed closer

& there is no return mother
not though you lie there forever

how much you wanted
that they might be
let into your time
a little while
          & sometimes were

you have become a box of dust
among grass & weeds
the small garden you lie in

your body compost .
the years you wrote for the Estevan Mercury
and now the last thing you wrote
your cremation creates the stars

I try to compose myself in composing you
your ashes fallen out of the stars
the small garden you lie in
turning to stars & grass
turning to blue
gamma

Dennis Cooley

IN THE SURROGATE COURT
FOR SASKATCHEWAN
JUDICIAL CENTRE OF REGINA

IN THE MATTER OF THE ESTATE OF
Irene June Cooley
Late of the City of Estevan,
in the Province of Saskatchewan,
Deceased.

FINAL RELEASE TO EXECUT

KNOW ALL MEN BY THESE PRESENTS that I Dennis Orin Cooley, of the City of Winnipeg, in the Province of Manitoba, Professor, DO HEREBY ACKNOWLEDGE that I have this day had and received from Dennis Orin Cooley of the City of Winnipeg, in the Province of Manitoba and Donald William. Kindopp, of the City of Estevan, in the Province of Saskatchewan, co-executors, of the Estate of Irene June Cooley, Deceased,

being my distribution of my share of the Estate of the Deceased;

AND THEREFORE I, the said Dennis Orin Cooley DO MY THESE PRESENTS, remise, release, quit claim and forever discharge the said Dennis Orin Cooley and Donald William Kindopp as aforesaid, their heirs, executors, and administrators of and from any claim for my said share in the said Estate.

IN WITNESS WHEREOF I have hereunto set my hand and seal this_____ day of_____A.D. 19   -

SIGNED, SEALED and DELIVERED)
by the said   )
in the presence of   )
)
_____) _____
Witness

Irene   75

anthology: a collection of flowers
book a vase then though i never
would have pressed flowers between pages
nor would you nor would either of us
    know who did but i knew
you put water into the yard and the yard turned into
a freckled place blue squeezed through

                    i know in may diane
                    crouches over the beds
            presses her breath into the holes
            covers it carefully & waits

            that a weed tumbled in from a back yard
            rolled its brittleness into your body
            blue & red you dreamed in
            rolled its bones into your back
            yard bumped against your summer
            shook thick & thistled seeds
            into the bed you blossomed in
            blew in a stinking & lumpy breath
            blew blood out of every tomato

            know that colours when they are wet
            slip diane puts slips
            in water begin to put down
            hairy roots take on green
            begin the swim to your doorway
            that you took the sun in too, darkening
            planets popped out of your hands

            that you huddled with summer
            the small trees of estevan
            the sky's long blowings
            moons wobbled through
                seething with birds
            you in the end seeing things
            a terrible white flower
                        its snow drains
            the garden of colour

Dennis Cooley

step through the door
everything there everything
     where it has always been

          even the pens by the phone
          paper you have written on
          notes you have written
          pinned to the board

IDEAL AUTOBODY
933 Edward St. • Estevan
"Insurance Claims Welcome"
All Work Guaranteed in Writing

          iron lung kicks on
          in the basement

     where in the chill are you
     what envelopes have you
     folded yourself into

          the coffee maker gasps for air
          as when you were here it did
          as you when you died did

          write this at the table
          for 30 years you wrote at

          your handwriting so silent
          on the paper your voice
          fallen into a hole voices
          never escape from

                    where are you
                         where
                    are you

     you are in the back yard gardening
     in the closet looking for things
     you have taken your smile
     it has never been closer to you
     you have taken it with you
          into another room, your voice too
so light it barely registers

Irene   77

everything in your mind
everything you are
in the fields unreeling
the fields in you trolling
the bright in the sky
this is your place
this is your home
you do not want to end
you do not want to leave
you have paid your way in
you want to stay
till the end
want to see
the brown that was your eyes

wind so fast you could feel it
but you cannot feel the earth
turning all the way to china
wind pushing into earth
alters on the way through
little bits knocked off , worn away
time passes through

the tide sucks out
drawing away leaving them there to dry
clouds move so fast they curdle

heart a filter words sink through
all we said
passes through like water, clouded

Dennis Cooley

early spring
the soft earth
old plants

in the garage
you put for later

the three zucchini

all winter
their curved greenness

wrapped in old blankets
three zucchini

babies frozen
on the floor

another night dream:

am a
tug boat

light falling, sticky
sticking on other boats
other boats sticking to it

beautiful boats
the white sun
floating towards

where did the voices live
when they were here
where in the flesh were they

people rose with them
warm & fluid

then they go
                drier   looser
once they have hung on the sun
after they are pressed
between days that flutter
under our thumb

clothes on a line   drying

there is the old gramma cooley
and the new gramma cooley
dana said when she was small
            in 1975 or so
and you wrote in 1971
                you hurt your leg
when they buried your mother
and he said
the man who thought
about these things said
            this was years and years ago
you are playing the old mother game
                        aren't you
            the mother is there and then
                she is

Dennis Cooley

not there
              you have run
          the gamut
     from gamete to gambit haven't you
     it is a childish thing you do
              you close your eyes and
     there she is
          open and she's gone

                    a game of blue gamma then
     the way the mother comes
                              and goes
       a fine grammar of delay
          you play

          the letters   you sent
          fell   month   after month
          a silence of snowflakes
          into our yard   your love
          your loneliness too
          the way we   fell out from under
          at times you sent   that too

          disguised it all   in talk
          what you wrote   gardens   neighbours
          family   weather   politics   work

and though we phoned   came home
never wrote back   almost never
& never once did I

          tell you what   I meant to, quite
          though I   know you knew

as you wrote   you did not know
cancer is a snow storm
a terrrible white
weed no one can cancel
it blows inside you and you are caught
in it you will perish of cold
die from white out

nor do you know
I will write this
when it is too late

mother the young
men say dying
all the young men crying
out for their mothers

Dennis Cooley

in the kitchen
the shadow is in
shadow it is still
on the walls you moved
we move within
shadows lie
over the floor
your life
a shadow
still turned on

years ago
you gave us daisies
we never
planted
& died
& you
wept when you saw them
dead

& it is again summer, mother
the day Canada began

> we will bury your ashes soon
> one year later, nearly
> & though it rains now
> it will not rain soon

> this is an extra step
> the one when you thought
> you were down the stairs
> and you weren't

the clock that hung on your wall
hangs now on ours its one
battery beats on silent as a heart
chips chips time off our lives now
works away tick by tick

> > by tick

> meticulous
we hang our heart on the wall
it keeps our time now too

before its face your face fell from
wondering where time had gone
why it would not tick for you

Dennis Cooley

it is July
we have come

glass sky
presses beans corn cucumbers tomatoes
out of the earth its sweet flesh
flowers under the window sun pushes
its face against

& there
beside the garage

poppies   volunteer poppies
my dad's word-"volunteer"
outline the board walk in your garden
green and red mother green and red

you should be here
your garden needs you
you should be coming in
from your garden now
the sun in you & on you
your shoulders your happiness
yourself warm as breathing
new bread from the oven

it is july mother it is sun
it is green the summer is
full with july everything
inbetween mother everything inbetween

June 6
that would have been your birthday
Irene June Wilson
it would have been a perfect summer
all this rain mother so much rain

cemetery
July 13,
arc of one year   july to july
when you knew   when we bury you

the ravines below the hill
                    hold water, greenness
          have not been this way
since we were small

          the sandy soil
                    —family graves
all the rooms they lie in forever
          under blue
                    grampa wilson
          where he took me
—was, what, ?six
                    this spot is for me
          here is one for your mother
                    how frightened i felt
                              & sick
          the birds flying over, in wind
letting winter out of their bones
there were birds and a uranium sky
and winds that would cling to their wings

                    : a wild grass
          purple flowers sideways
          half feathers on the stem
patches of it, cemetery spotted with it
                    , its delicacy
          small modest blossoms
"blue gamma" Lorne says when Diane holds it up
     "gramma too"
                    /"blue gramma"

                    Dana moves off
          this is not her gramma
          the one she knows is nowhere
          in the service the minister

new from down East is young
never knew her
seeks to say what cannot be said
says what millions have said
& will say

my uncle Oris turned 85 into a place
memory has left
time has led him into a bewildered face
Ann what are we doing here he says
what are we doing here Ann

soil sandy as ever
gravel gathers by every grave the trees
try to drink
on top of the hill
but they
hardly breathe
how hard it must be for them to breathe
wind all summer the weight of sun
presses them to density
small birds call & tumble in wind

in winter hold themselves close
the hardly ever of their small lives

you at the end of the line shake
summer out in a stiff blue
swallows follow themselves through
messages twisted in the DNA of their feet
the new-born rain where you pinned
sunlight to the line & june happened

sky now
a stomach
& in it
a lime sun
burning

Irene

the same, almost
except the stillness
your clothes
the same, but not

hang there still
no longer clothes
air has shifted the room
feels as if
it had just moved

you have slipped away
from them you have slipt
them off &
left

them inside
where they clink
against one another
emptiness hangs
upside down

something like
a purple flower
that is not
there

in the kitchen
the shadow
is still
turned on

Dennis Cooley

ashes to ashes he says
dust to dust
the stars you fell from fell into
the garden your body becomes
your cremation creates the stars
yes this is true
so true we can weep

but where   in the words
do we open   any life
who speaks   the small
sweet moment   between

are you
mother
small planet of dust

the air fallen away, its shakings
everything you said, gathered
stones you skipped across water
& sunk

& who will weep for us when we die

the silences of these pages
birds
in winter
drifting

the small garden you lie in
turning to grass
turning to blue gamma

Irene

where are you where
have you gone mother
where have they put your teasings
perhaps they put them out for awhile
and even now they are scratching at the door

they are not in the afternoon I look into
they never are though I find myself looking

where has your voice fallen have you
misplaced it somewhere and forgotten
where the warmth your body found and kept
what has happened to it what has happened

the thumb with the nail
divided so evenly someone
could have measured where
is the ridge now where
shall I tell your garden you have gone
you have gone
for a walk & you have
taken your talk with you

where in things have you gone
what accident have you fallen into

what has happened mother
what has happened to you

around us the world falls
a soft and invisible snowfall we do not see
a winter we do not wake from, quite, or ever

Dennis Cooley

bodies are
tubers put into darkness
darkness blots up time
you cannot peel off like tape

darkness could be a worker
taking up old carpets
POP **POP** POP POP
flesh unsnapped from bones

voices dissolve in soil
wash away in rain words as if they never were
spoken before as they never will again
not though we call till we can speak no more

all we know is
time for a time hangs

the sweet flesh   hums
bright fish   feeding at coral

and then
millions & millions of voices
run away
go to the sea back to the waters back into sun
a moment exhaled on breath
all the voices flesh & bone have made

nothing we can say
can rinse the darkness off
talk flesh back into time
the yard calling
rooms crying out
children talking
taking their time
the few moments we have
to swing on our bones

huge bedroom
all these people
sleeping together
who when they were living
would never have dreamt
or having dreamt never thought
or having thought never done

such a thing
taken rooms in the same windy apartment
everybody cozied up   like this
snuggling   /practically
stone pillows their heads lie forever under
the whole town the whole species
a crazy intimacy of smugglers
they have sneaked past borders carrying
on like that, drowsing in stone pastures

crows in all that time drone by like fat flies

old familiars new neighbours buzz & gossip
till the hill sounds
infested with grasshoppers

can hear you now
among dry grass & flowers
, laughing

Dennis Cooley

hear you
    Sharon & Lynn
& then you

downstairs talking

    it is 1962
i am away at university
    18 and homesick
but i am in bed in Winnipeg
    it is Nov 29, 1992

    & in the dream i can
        hear you
    downstairs, talking

in this dream
you lay your
head on my shoulder
or i lay mine on yours

it is april 6, 1993

your voice is gentle
& husky

Dennis Cooley

yes it is mother
                                winter
        light on wood
        the unshoved air

        a room that answers
the window light
        the fresh snow
                the paper
        boy has marked
    blue flowers   ,bruises
                where he's walked

        the snow the light
                the new
        year's quiet

you said

you said

Dennis Cooley

it is christmas day
           , 1995
the snow is bright

      we shine & cook
             the smell of the tree
      sweetens the house
         loosens the day the
  fresh coffee i always take milk in a blessing

         the round glass
         bright as the sun
           we clean & hang
      in the kitchen window
           the purple flowers
        we gave you in it
         their colours fading
)hand mirror you cleaned with your breath

          it turns very
                      slowly
            a bright circle
   it could be a bird
      bright as the sun
        on the end of
           the fishing
        line a beautiful
      bruise in the light

you should see it mother
      5 years later
           the light is still
                      there

Feb 1.96

startled this morning
-41° a bitter winter
day after day a cold bright sun

shocked to think you are the mother whose garden dies
never reflowers whose daughter never returns
the woman whose word is carried off in winter's arms
i had the flowers, yes, but not this
story in my head

peace it says Eirene   Irene June
was the spirit of spring one of the three
or four there were sometimes four sometimes two
for the greeks there was no fall
spring summer and winter the Horae the Seasons the Hours
the Seasons had little mythology the book says though
there was the other woman we all know who loved
flowers was gathering flowers in a meadow. Perhaps
a garden. She found crocuses irises hyacinths
purple flowers though there were roses too and lilies.
No lilacs. They lacked lilacs. She found a crocus
she especially liked but when she picked it
you know the story the earth opened

and out of it a man
/rose
he may have been dressed in white
a snow man you could say

a cold man
and he took her off
to a dark place

Dennis Cooley

There are no flowers only her mother
frantic goes in search and now she returns
they say every spring when grass is brown and trees are pickled.
Empty books of hours hands full of seeds birds trickle from.
But she is tricked she has eaten the fruit so every fall
she goes back to the cold dark place.

       Hades, a place of shade.
       A cold dark pantry.
       utterly inhospitable

There were no flowers anywhere then. It was winter.

You would have liked this, mother.
Eirene an eiron. You would have teased.

       People worry one time she might not
   come back might be gone forever and ever
          might forget where she is
             there where it is
        so cool and so shady and
           never return.

      They might be hungry without her
       and there would be no crops
  and the world would be leafless and bare,
       they might sing of her.

     good night Irene
     good night Irene
     I'll see you
     in my dreams.

                he said the other man
                the man from the dark
             & the man from home

   The Horae "attend
the greater deities and provide
attractive decoration
in literature and art"—

there is nothing
any one can say
or ever say
when you are dead
& you are dead
beyond all fields & rocks
beyond all the stones in the field

under stone flowers stuck by your head
planted in wobbly rows
each sun collapsing
an emptied lung
memory dropping off
all the words worn away
the letters too silent
that mark your box of dust
the whole world itself burnt
past recognition before it began

there is nothing
past where it began
there is nothing
to say
when you are dead to say
you are dead
you are dead

Dennis Cooley

mirror in our upstairs hall
near which we've slept
we pass waking to sleeping
sleeping to waking flowers
cut into its edges & in it
or grass it could be grass
where every morning we rise

mirror mirror in the hall where is
but no you remember shining it for Christmas
Dec 10.97 see it in full light
you were thinking of the other one
its light to a northern wind
     a winter garden

in it from time to time our faces
where once was yours
        appear & disappear
      brief moments of light & shadow
  dianes megans danas mine
slip off where we've been
& Dana's in two weeks will return
      what we were   /are

        quick flowers
      light & dark
         our living
  room   /yours dads
sharons lynns   mine   laurels
        we were quick

  silver behind the glass
     for 40 years we slipt
  ghosts past the glass
        our faces in winter
  now flower whitely in

Irene

in the spring
        i would find them
south end of the pasture
over the hill i imagined
people standing for 10,000 years
faces to the wind
the snow not melted in spots

the wiry thick grass
dad said was native
dusty and dry much of the summer

their fuzzy clumps
        eight or nine at a time
            the thick root
    driven into the hillside

        pale blue or mauve
sometimes they were there
                into september

Dennis Cooley

DATE DUE

Apr. 30 '08	